HELEN COOPER

Helen Cooper was born and brought up in The Hague, Holland, of Welsh/Dutch parentage.

Her plays include *Mrs Gauguin*, finalist Susan Smith Blackburn Award (Almeida Theatre, London; Amsterdam; Hamburg; Ghent), *Mrs Vershinin*, finalist Susan Smith Blackburn Award (Riverside Studios, London; Tramway, Glasgow; Theater der Welt, Hamburg; broadcast on BBC Radio 3), and *The House of Ruby Moon*, developed by the Royal National Theatre Studio and premiered at the London New Play Festival.

Her translations include *Miss Julie* for Greenwich Theatre, *Hedda Gabler* for Chichester Festival Theatre, and *Don Giovanni* for Scottish Opera. Her radio plays include *Mothers At The Gate*. Her screenplay of *Miss Julie* was directed by Mike Figgis, featuring Saffron Burrows and Peter Mullan. Her highly acclaimed short film, *Station*, which she wrote and produced (directed by Jackie Oudney), was nominated as Best Short Film for BAFTA Scotland's New Talent Award.

Her acting credits range from contemporary work with Hull Truck, the Bush Theatre, the Royal Court and the ICA to classical work at the Crucible Theatre, Sheffield and the Old Vic, London.

She has completed the screenplay *Antonia* for Amica Films and is working on a commission for Hampstead Theatre. She lives in London with director/writer Mike Bradwell and their daughter Flora.

Other Titles in this Series

Helen Cooper

THREE WOMEN AND A PIANO TUNER

NICK HERN BOOKS
London
www.nickhernbooks.co.uk

A Nick Hern Book

Three Women and a Piano Tuner first published in Great Britain as a paperback original in 2004 by Nick Hern Books Limited, 14 Larden Road, London W3 7ST.

Three Women and a Piano Tuner copyright © 2004 Helen Cooper

Helen Cooper has asserted her right to be identified as the author of this work

Cover Image: Clare Park

Typeset by Country Setting, Kingsdown, Kent CT14 8ES
Printed and bound in Great Britain by Cox and Wyman Ltd, Reading, Berks

A CIP catalogue record for this book is available from the British Library

ISBN 1 85459 814 7

For
Mike and Flora

Three Women and a Piano Tuner was first performed at the
Minerva Theatre, Chichester, on 3 June 2004 (previews from
28 May), with the following cast:

ELLA	Jane Gurnett
BETH	Suzanne Burden
LIZ	Eleanor David
HAROLD	Gareth David-Lloyd

Director Samuel West
Designer Ashley Martin-Davis
Composer Jason Carr
Lighting Designer Peter Mumford
Sound Designer Scott George
Movement Director Michael Ashcroft

The author would like to thank Verena Lewis, Jason Osborn,
Steven Pimlott, Evelyn Preston, Paul Sirett, Samuel West,
the Kensington Library and Graziana's Café.

Characters

in order of appearance

ELLA, *a woman of around forty*

BETH, *a woman of around forty*

LIZ, *a woman of around forty*

HAROLD, *a young man of around twenty*

ACT ONE

A piano is being tuned.

The lights fade up on a studio/kitchen. The walls and floors are covered with books, paintings, CDs, records, papers and manuscript books.

The sound of the piano being tuned comes from a room next door.

ELLA *comes in, followed by* BETH. *Both are wrapped up in winter coats.*

ELLA *switches on a light.* BETH *stays hovering in the doorway.* ELLA *looks at* BETH *standing there for a while.* BETH *looks at her.*

ELLA
It will take a while to warm up so keep your coat on.

BETH
Yes.

ELLA *switches on an electric heater.*

ELLA
Sit down.

BETH *sits down at the kitchen table.*

BETH
Thank you.

ELLA *looks at* BETH *sitting at the table for a while.* BETH *looks at her.*

ELLA *walks to a cupboard and takes four glasses out and brings them to the table.*

BETH
(*looking around her*)
It's nice.

ELLA
Thank you, you're generous.

BETH
No, I'm not. It's nice.

ELLA
Thank you. Red?

BETH
I'd better stick to white.

ELLA
Red is better for you . . . full of iron –

ELLA *gets the wine and comes back to the table with a bottle of white wine, which has already been opened and half-drunk. She takes the cork out and pours two glasses.*

ELLA
Liz shouldn't be long now.

BETH
Good.

ELLA *joins* BETH *at the kitchen table, choosing the chair that is furthest away from* BETH. *There is a tension between them.* ELLA *looks at* BETH.

ELLA
To you.

BETH
To you.

They sip their drinks. Pause.

ELLA
I'm sorry, the food . . . Those beans . . .

BETH *looks at* ELLA.

ELLA
Tinned . . .

BETH
I suppose they were.

ELLA
And the fish was still frozen in the centre . . .

BETH
I wasn't hungry anyway.

ELLA
We shouldn't have paid.

BETH
You shouldn't have paid.

ELLA
I wanted to treat you.

BETH
Thank you, that was nice.

ELLA *looks at her watch.*

ELLA
The wine was good though.

BETH
It was.

ELLA
And beans don't lose their goodness after having been tinned.

BETH
Don't they?

ELLA
No, they don't. Nor does fish lose its goodness after having
been frozen.

BETH
I didn't know that.

ELLA
They continue to nourish.

BETH
I never really thought about it.

ELLA

It's good to know though, don't you think?

BETH

Yes.

ELLA

I like fish. Fish and chips and ketchup.

ELLA *looks at* BETH *and studies her reaction. There is little.*

The piano tuning continues. They both listen to it.

ELLA
(*referring to the piano tuner*)
He's not blind.

BETH

No? That's unusual.

ELLA

It is, isn't it? No, he can see very well.

BETH

Good.

ELLA

And he's young.

BETH
(*surprised*)
Ah . . .

ELLA

He is. Very.

ELLA *smiles at* BETH, *who smiles back.* ELLA *studies* BETH's *reaction.*

ELLA

It's funny what you were saying about you forgetting . . .

BETH *gets a packet of cigarettes out of her bag.*

BETH

Do you mind?

ELLA

No, go ahead. I don't mind.

BETH *lights a cigarette.*

ELLA

. . . because I was thinking . . . I remember just before my father died, he suddenly clutched my head with both his hands and pulled my head towards his and I laughed and bowed my head and wrenched it free from him.

Pause.

ELLA

It just took a fraction of a second, but it was a moment I remembered again and again and again. First, frantically, every moment of the day, then only at night time before falling asleep, then once a week maybe, then twice a year until it lost its power to intoxicate and it had no use to be remembered – and that's when I forgot it.

BETH

Just before he died?

ELLA

Yes.

BETH *thinks about this.*

BETH

Intoxicate?

ELLA

Yes.

BETH

I'm sorry, have you got an ashtray?

ELLA

Yes, of course.

ELLA *gets up to get an ashtray and brings it back to the table.*

BETH

But you do remember it.

ELLA

Only now, to illustrate the process of forgetting.

BETH

I see. So you haven't forgotten it.

ELLA

Because you reminded me of it.

BETH

So it hasn't gone.

ELLA

Gone where?

BETH *thinks about it but has no answer. She shrugs her shoulders.*

ELLA

Exactly. Where is there for it to go?

BETH

(*not seeing*)
I see.

Pause.

BETH

William always says: 'The past is not dead, it isn't even past.'

ELLA

(*surprised*)
Does he?

Pause. BETH *stubs out her cigarette, which she has hardly smoked.*

BETH

I shouldn't really. I'm trying to give up.

ELLA *raises her glass.*

ELLA

To you! Thank you for coming.

BETH

No. Thank you for asking me.

They sip their wine.

> BETH
> (*about the wine*)
> This is nice.

> ELLA
> Thank you. You're generous.

They sip.

> ELLA
> Liz was sure you wouldn't come tonight.

> BETH
> Why?

> ELLA
> I think she felt you had moved on.

> BETH
> Me? If anyone has, it's Liz who has moved on. It's much more likely she won't come tonight.

> ELLA
> No, Liz is committed to this project. She'll be here.

> BETH
> Good.

BETH *opens her packet of cigarettes then closes it again.*

> BETH
> She's looking very well still, isn't she?

> ELLA
> Who?

> BETH
> Liz.

> ELLA
> Have you seen her? I thought you hadn't seen each other for all these years. When did you see her? She said she hadn't seen you for all these years. She said that she was looking forward to seeing you again after all these years. When did you see her?

BETH
. . . No, I haven't seen her. Only in magazines and newspapers.

ELLA
Oh . . . I see . . . Yes . . . Of course.
Liz is good at blowing her own shiny trumpet.

They sip their wine.

ELLA
And I?

BETH
Sorry?

ELLA
Do I look well?

BETH
Ah . . . yes.

ELLA *looks at* BETH. *She obviously wants more.*

BETH
Yes, you do look well. Very well.

ELLA
As well as Liz?

BETH
I don't know. I haven't seen Liz. Only in the magazines and
newspapers. Yes, you do look well.

ELLA rearranges her own hair.

ELLA
So do you.

BETH
No, I don't. You don't need to say I do because I know I don't.
Don't worry. I don't mind.

ELLA
You do look well. Your skin is soft. Your hair is shiny. Your
nails and teeth are strong. Your cashmere coat, your Prada
shoes . . .

BETH *strokes her cashmere coat with slight*
embarrassment.

ELLA

I'm not suggesting that you took the easy route because I know
now that there isn't one. But don't you miss the music?

BETH

No, I don't. Life is too busy now.

They listen to the piano tuner who is indulging in a little
prelude.

ELLA

Sounds different, doesn't it, now you know that he's not blind,
that he can see?

BETH

Yes.

ELLA

And that he's young.

BETH

Yes.

ELLA *sips her wine.*

BETH

I can't stay long.

ELLA

Why not?

BETH

William . . .

ELLA

Ah, yes, of course.

BETH *smiles apologetically.*

ELLA

Yes, well . . . maybe I should get on with it. I'm sorry Liz is
late. That's what fame has done to her. She has no regard for
time. She just uses and abuses it.

BETH

I hate wasting it.

ELLA

What?

BETH

Time. I always try to save it.

ELLA

Of course you do.

BETH

Then once I've saved it, I don't know how to kill it.

ELLA

What?

BETH

Time.

ELLA

You strangle it.

ELLA *strangles Time.*

ELLA

Like this.

ELLA *wipes her hands on her skirt.*

ELLA

I wash my hands of it. I wash my hands of it.

BETH *shivers.*

The piano tuner has gone back to tuning.

ELLA

Where was I before we left the restaurant?

BETH

In the restaurant.

ELLA

What?

BETH

That's where you were.

ELLA
No . . .

ELLA   BETH
No, I mean . . .   I know, I know, let's see . . .

They both try to remember.

BETH
The oblong table.

ELLA

Oh, yes, of course, the oblong table. Every evening meal at six o'clock exactly. Every evening. And I was always worrying whether Mother would be in a good mood or not. She always was when there were guests, but when there weren't, it was grim for her to face the cruel facts: a man without ambition, four mediocre daughters, her own wild talent shrivelled up, no money, a damp, small, rented house. Even after she had covered all the cushions in desperate florals and painted the room, we ate in a deep blue, it never could pretend to be what it was not.

BETH *looks at her diamond ring.*

ELLA

But when a guest did eat with us, then Mother's hair had curls, her lips were red, her eyes had pale blue eye-shadow. There would be alcohol and so the atmosphere would be completely different.

Then Mother would forget that her eldest daughter was considered thick, no school could teach her, that number two had a nasty temper and tendencies to mingle with a dodgy crowd, that the youngest, the mute one, slouching in a corner, simply would not eat or drink or speak and that Jane, number three, had given up playing the piano, because she felt she was grotesque, too ugly to perform in public, too off-putting to be looked at, to be seen. Jane kept begging Mother for all mirrors in the house to be removed, and finally, one day, Mother shrugged her aching shoulders in despair and stored all mirrors in the coalhole.

BETH *lights another cigarette.*

ELLA

Couldn't Mother have prevented it? Jane's death? Couldn't she have prevented it? And what about Father?

ELLA *waits for a reaction from* BETH. *But there is none.*

ELLA

We all knew that Father's life was not around that oblong table. It was elsewhere but only I knew where. That was the secret and I guarded it. I knew that Mother didn't know I knew, but I knew that she suspected that I knew and I knew that that was bad enough. So I kept my mouth firmly shut and hardly ever ate or drank or spoke in the presence of my mother.

ELLA *looks at* BETH *smoking.*

ELLA

Mother always was embarrassed when she was asked what Father's profession was. 'He plays . . . eh . . . the viola *(embarrassed laugh)* in a small orchestra.'

BETH *does not react.*

ELLA

Couldn't Mother have prevented it?

BETH *does not react.*

ELLA

And yet how could it have been her fault? She tried. She always tried. She cooked and cleaned and washed and sewed. She made us practise the piano, practice, practice . . . Four daughters to bring up on the income from just one small viola in a feeble orchestra.

But of course after Jane's death, after we had all been kicked out of our oblivion and been woken up to the terror of reality, our previous poverty seemed rich.

Especially for Mother; 'Before the Fall' became a beautiful glowing island of our intimate togetherness, a kind of haven before we were all forced to sail the unknown seas.

Right up until her death, old and decrepit as she was, Mother still hankered back to that blissful paradise. But I was there, don't forget, the mute one, slouching in the corner, and I can tell you, blissful it was not.

BETH *waits for more.*

ELLA

You see, that is the recurring theme. Around that oblong table every night at six o'clock.

BETH
I see.

ELLA

But what it is about – the heart of it – is the man who was elsewhere.

BETH
The father.

ELLA
Yes. The man with no ambition.

BETH *shivers and stubs her cigarette out.*

ELLA
Shall I turn the heat up?

BETH *gets up.*

BETH
No, thank you, I must go.

ELLA
You can't.

ELLA *takes a sip of wine.*

BETH *looks at ELLA.*

ELLA *smiles at BETH.*

ELLA
Beth . . . you know you can't.

BETH *looks powerless.*

ELLA
Sit down, relax, and I shall turn the heat up.

ELLA *turns the heat up.*

BETH *sits down reluctantly.*

ELLA

After all, who paid for dinner?

BETH *has no answer to that.*

ELLA

Exactly.

ELLA *pours herself another glass of wine.*

ELLA

The Stork.

BETH *looks apprehensive.*

ELLA

One day, Father told me that he'd heard a stork had come back, after years, to a long-deserted stork's nest, a rubber tyre on top of a high pole.

BETH

Where?

ELLA

It was miles away, near the lake. We set off together, just the two of us, one Sunday morning. We drove there together, just him and me.

BETH

How old were you?

ELLA

Thirteen. He parked the car where we could see the nest without disturbing it. It was a deserted lane. And there we sat in the parked car, close together, waiting for the stork. His binoculars were lying in his lap. Not many words were spoken. 'Storks are voiceless or nearly so,' he said, 'but some of them chatter their bills loudly when excited. They fly flapping and soaring, flapping and soaring with their necks outstretched and their legs trailing.'

BETH

Just the two of you?

ELLA

Yes. Every bird that came our way, he would point out to me. It wasn't what he pointed out that stirred me, but how; his left arm around me like a wing, covering the whole of me, his right arm reaching far out of the window and with his hand, with the middle finger of his hand, he pointed out the birds to me. He knew every name of every bird we saw. The heron was my favourite.

BETH
Stirred?

ELLA
Yes . . . how would you describe it?

BETH *thinks about it.*

BETH
I don't know.

ELLA

Mostly, Father and I were silent and that was alright. We could have stayed there for eternity for all I cared. It was *all* right. Our minds wandered off in different directions, then turned round and met up again. Then we would speak out, simultaneously. 'Are you hungry?' in unison, then silence. 'How much longer shall we give it?' in unison, then silence. 'Shall we have fish and chips and ketchup on the way back?'

BETH
Did you?

ELLA

We did. We didn't eat Mother's sandwiches. We waited until dark. The stork never showed himself.

ELLA *pours more wine.*

BETH
Why are you telling me all this?

ELLA
Because it is important.

BETH
So what's the punchline?

ELLA
The stork never showed himself.

BETH
No. The punchline.

ELLA
Ah . . .
(*she smiles*)
Death?

ELLA *takes her coat off.*

ELLA
Beth, please. We haven't even started yet.
So relax. Take off your coat.

BETH *unbuttons her coat and opens it a little.*

It is quiet now. We don't hear any tuning.

ELLA
The knife.

BETH
What knife?

ELLA
With the carved handle. Like a little dagger.

BETH *can't remember.*

ELLA
We gave it to Jane for her twelfth birthday.
A knife to carve wood with. It was exactly what she wanted.

BETH
A little dagger?

ELLA
Yes. It vanished.

BETH *can't remember.*

ELLA
For her birthday we went for a picnic on the island, the island
in the lake. We loved that island, that's where we always went.
Then during the picnic, we hid her brand new dagger.

BETH
Why?

ELLA
To trick her.

BETH
Did we?

ELLA

We did, we did. But the strange thing is, that it was never found again. It vanished. Disappeared. We looked everywhere. We searched until dark. Jane was distraught.

The following week, I confided in Father, just like he always confided in me. And we went back together to the island in the lake, just him and me, to look for it.

Hand in hand, we searched the island. How old are you when you're too old to hold your father's hand?

BETH
That depends.

ELLA

I left my hand in his. Later on, when we were tired, we lay down together in the grass, my head resting on his chest.

BETH *is uncomfortable.*

ELLA

He knew every name of every star we saw. I could hear his voice reverberating in his chest as he told me stories of how the sun and moon sometimes eclipse each other; how, when the sun is eclipsed by the moon to us, the earth is eclipsed by the moon to the sun.

He told me about the forces that make the waters of the seas swell until they burst unlike the waters of our lake . . . until eventually we fell asleep. We never found the knife.

BETH *smoothes out the creases in her skirt. She gets up, then sits down again.*

ELLA

You see, there is a pattern: the stork who never showed himself,
the dagger never found, the shoes he never bought, the swordfish that was dead; but what mattered was the stalking of the
stork, the searching for the dagger, the looking for the shoes,
the hunting for the swordfish, the swimming in the sea, the
swimming in the lake, the laughter in the dark, and when we
were locked up, and we could hear the crying . . .

LIZ has materialised in the room. She stands there,
wrapped up in her winter coat, slightly in a daze.

ELLA

How long have you been there?

Pause.

LIZ

Harold let me in . . .

LIZ unbuttons her coat and takes it off.

LIZ

It's hot in here.

ELLA

You've met Harold . . . ?

Pause.

LIZ

Yes . . .

ELLA

And?

ELLA and LIZ look at each other for quite a while.

ELLA

What do you think?

LIZ

I don't know.

ELLA

What did he say?

LIZ

Well, he's not exactly going to be ecstatic, is he, meeting me?

ELLA

No, I suppose not. What did he say?
Did you talk to each other? What did you say?

LIZ

What is there to say?

ELLA

Yes . . . I see . . .

BETH

Who's Harold?

LIZ *turns to* BETH.

BETH *gets up.*

LIZ

Beth . . . ?

LIZ *looks at* BETH.

BETH *looks at* LIZ, *embarrassed.*

BETH

Yes . . .

They look at each other for a while.

ELLA *looks at them looking at each other.*

LIZ

(*to* BETH)
Have you met Harold?

ELLA

No, not yet. She hasn't yet.

BETH

Who's Harold?

Pause. LIZ *looks at* ELLA.

ELLA

The piano tuner.

Pause.

LIZ
He's very beautiful.

ELLA *beams.*

ELLA
He is, isn't he? I haven't asked Beth yet.
I wanted to wait until you were here.

LIZ
I need a drink.

ELLA
Oh yes, of course.

LIZ
(*to* BETH)
It's been so long. You look well.

BETH
Don't! I don't. Don't worry. I don't mind. It's good to see you.

ELLA
Would you like some wine? We're drinking white.

LIZ
I'd like red.

ELLA *moves to the cupboard.*

ELLA
It's better for you. Full of iron.

LIZ *joins* BETH *at the table, but keeps her distance.*

The piano tuner has started to tune again.

BETH
(*to* LIZ)
You've done well.

LIZ
Not bad, not bad. And you. A millionaire husband,
three tidy mansions, and no overdraft . . .

ELLA

She's very generous.

LIZ

(*to* ELLA)

She can afford to be.

(*to* BETH)

Two children neatly tucked away at boarding school . . .

ELLA

They're William's.

LIZ

What?

ELLA

They're William's children.

LIZ

Ah.

(*to* BETH)

Look at your hands! Your skin! So soft . . .

(*to* ELLA)

Look, her hands! Her skin! So soft . . .

LIZ *keeps looking at them.*

LIZ

I remember them. They haven't changed at all. They're lovely.

BETH

They're not.

LIZ

They are! Look, Ella! Idle hands!

ELLA *joins them at the table and studies* BETH's *hands.*

ELLA

Mine have shrivelled.

She puts her hands on the table.

BETH

They haven't.

> LIZ
> I see what you mean . . .

> ELLA
> Have they?

LIZ *puts her hands on the table.* BETH *and* ELLA *look at them.*

> BETH
> (*to* LIZ)
> Your hands are wonderful, they radiate.
> They seem to glow with light.

> ELLA
> Because they're worshipped!

BETH *and* LIZ *look at* ELLA.

> ELLA
> Even cows glow with light as long as they are worshipped.

> LIZ
> Sorry?

> ELLA
> Sacred cows are worshipped and so they glow with light.

> LIZ
> Ah . . . but does a cow glow with light because she is
> worshipped or is she worshipped because she glows with light?

ELLA *does not answer.*

BETH *senses the tension between* LIZ *and* ELLA.

> BETH
> (*to* LIZ)
> Don't worry, your hands are beautiful.

> LIZ
> (*to* ELLA)
> She IS generous.

> ELLA
> She is.

BETH
(*still looking at* LIZ's *hands*)
To think that they're world-famous now.

ELLA
Odes have been dedicated to them.
Critics have waxed lyrically over them.

LIZ
And condemned them to death.

ELLA
Hardly.

LIZ
Often. They've often died and were reborn.

BETH
They've grown. I swear they've grown!

ELLA *measures them by comparing them to her own.*

ELLA
They have, you know. They have grown about an inch.

LIZ
What do you expect?

BETH
Are they insured?

LIZ
Of course.

BETH
How much?

ELLA
A lot, I bet.

BETH
How much?

LIZ
For what they're worth.

ELLA
A lot.

LIZ
A lot.
(*to* BETH)
Like the ring you're wearing.

They all admire BETH's *wedding ring.*

LIZ
How much is that insured for?

BETH *shrugs her shoulders.*

LIZ
A lot – I bet.

ELLA
(*gently waving her right hand*)
This is the hand, that shook the hand, that shook the hand of Tippet.

The others don't like this memory.

LIZ	BETH
(*flicking her right hand as if it has been burnt*)	(*cradling her right hand as if it has been hurt*)
OH, NO.	AH . . . NO.

LIZ
Where is my wine? It's hot in here.

LIZ *takes another piece of clothing off.*

ELLA
Beth feels the cold.

ELLA *leaves the table to open the bottle of red wine for* LIZ.

The piano tuner indulges in a wild burst of music. They all listen.

LIZ
Not bad.

ELLA
(*proud*)
Not bad, is it?

LIZ *turns to* BETH.

LIZ
So what do you think?

BETH
About what?

LIZ
Ella's proposal?

ELLA *takes a sip of wine.*

BETH
What proposal?

ELLA
No, I haven't told her yet. I wanted to wait until you were here.

LIZ
Well, I'm here!

BETH
I can't stay long.

LIZ
Why not?

BETH
William . . .

LIZ
I see.

ELLA
Let me just get you your wine.

ELLA *gets a bottle of wine out of the cupboard and starts opening it.*

LIZ
(*to* BETH)
So what is William like? Does he wear flannel trousers, brogues, blazers, boxer shorts and ties . . . ?

BETH *looks at* LIZ, *but does not answer.*

LIZ

Does he bring you to the boil until you whistle?

BETH *has no answer.*

LIZ

Has he ever? Sometimes?
Or are you still hoping against hope that one day maybe he will?

BETH *has no answer.*

LIZ

Does he enhance your beauty or diminish it?
Do you like wearing him when you go out?
Or do you shine brighter without that particular accessory?
Does he function?

BETH *has no answer.*

LIZ

Does he still hear you? Does he listen? Does he play you well?
Did he ever or are you still hoping against hope that maybe
one day he will?

Does he punish you? Do you have to pay? Does he wound you
deeply where it hurts, the way only true lovers can and
mothers with their children?

Does he hate you with desire? Does he want to knife you
where it kills? Does he feel the need to torture you? Has he
ever? Or are you hoping against all hope that one day maybe
he will?

BETH *has no answer.*

LIZ

Would he give his life for you? Would he sacrifice his children
to rescue you, does he want to keep you from all harm?
Does he dream with you or alone? Does he exist? Do you
know him?

Can you smell him when he isn't there? Can you hear him?
Does his smell always please you? Sometimes or never at all?
Are you still listening? Does his flesh make you weep with
desire? Did it ever? Or are you hoping against all hope that one
day maybe it will?

Do you want to dig your nails deep into his skin, then tear his flesh off only to kiss it better? Do you want to bite his cock off, spit it out then gently cradle his mutilated body in your loving arms until he, sobbing, falls asleep?

Do you love him?

Pause.

BETH
It's not as simple as all that.

Pause.

LIZ
No, of course it isn't. No, of course not.

ELLA *comes to the table and pours a glass of red wine for* LIZ.

BETH *lights another cigarette.*

ELLA
She doesn't miss the music.
Her life is far too busy now.

BETH
I still have my piano stool, my metronome and my old manuscript books.

But no, I don't miss it because I can afford to go and listen to the best. I know I'm spoilt. Everyone who looks at me sees a rich woman. Everyone who hears my married name knows my husband is a multi-millionaire. That is my visiting card.

We live a very pleasant life in our three tidy mansions. The children are at boarding school, our staff clean up behind us and satisfy our whims. Our whims are modest. We entertain. We go to the opera, to concerts and the theatre. We travel when and where we want to. William is content . . .

But, yes, you're right. I am still hoping against all hope . . . but isn't everyone?

One day, I knocked on William's chest . . .

I peeped in . . .

Raised up the latch . . .

Walked in . . .

And found me, sitting there quite comfortably.

Pause.

ELLA
That's good . . . that's very good . . .

LIZ
You were sitting? Not lying, naked with your legs apart?

BETH
No, sitting, quite comfortably.

LIZ
Not bad . . . not bad . . . And have you ever heard what happened to your baby boy you gave up for adoption? He must be a young man by now.

BETH *freezes.*

ELLA *and* LIZ *look at her.*

BETH
No, no, William doesn't know, I've never told him – I've never told a soul . . . I tried once . . . once, to contact him, through . . . an agency, but I was told that he didn't want to know . . . so I must respect that . . . but he is alive . . . I know that . . . He is alive . . .

No-one speaks for a while. The tuning is coming to an end.

They all sip their wine.

BETH
Ella was the bravest, really.

LIZ
Yes, Ella was the bravest.

ELLA
I don't know – was I?

LIZ *is hot. She takes another piece of clothing off.*

LIZ
(*to* ELLA)
You better ask her now.

BETH *is hot, but only unbuttons another button of her coat.*

BETH
I can't stay long . . .

ELLA
Well, what it all boils down to is that beautiful creature . . . that core . . . that throbbing pump that motors us along . . .

Neither LIZ *nor* BETH *knows quite what this is leading to.*

ELLA
. . . but then there comes a time . . . when we forget why those glorious pumps keep pumping. That is despair . . . However . . . no-one, no island, no lake, no sea, no star, no swordfish, no stork, no child, no woman, no man knows why. And yet, deep inside us, we feel we could find out if we really tried . . . and . . . if that is so, if we could find out, if we CAN know, surely it would be intolerable not to.

BETH
Sorry . . . ?

ELLA
You see, you can detect the search for 'why' in every man-made wonder: a spaceship, a microchip, a well-cut diamond, a perfect pirouette.

BETH *and* LIZ *look at* ELLA.

ELLA
As I see it, we are divided. First, there are those who know it is their task to simply service the almighty pump at all cost and keep it well maintained, well oiled, every nut and bolt in place, repairing parts that are exhausted and replacing parts that have conked out . . . then there are those whose task it is to find out WHY we keep this pump so smoothly running. What is driving us to sacrifice all our energy and imagination to keep that pump from grinding to a final halt?

Neither BETH *nor* LIZ *have an answer.*

ELLA

Now some of us have intimations that the answer is as simple, as complex, as magnificent as the slog itself. Because some of us suspect that that is the answer. There lies the treasure we are all hunting for: the slog itself . . . There is no there . . .

Pause.

LIZ takes another piece of clothing off.

BETH
You've lost me.

LIZ puts her hand on ELLA's glass that is still half-full.

LIZ
I think you've had enough.

ELLA *looks at* LIZ.

LIZ
Just tell her why she's here.

ELLA
If I could tell her that, if anyone could tell her that . . .

LIZ
As in: 'Here in your kitchen', not 'Here on Earth'.

ELLA
Ah, oh I see, yes.

ELLA *turns to* BETH.

ELLA
(*to* BETH)
I have composed a piano concerto.

BETH *takes this in.*

BETH
I thought you'd given up.

ELLA
I've spent ten years on it. It's finished. There it is.

ELLA *points to a large bundle of manuscript papers in a wooden box, then she gets up and picks it up.*

ELLA

(*holding the box and contents*)

My only dream now is to hear this and for this to be
heard and understood. And that's why we are here.

ELLA *holds the box up to* BETH.

LIZ *and* ELLA *look at* BETH.

LIZ

I have agreed to play the piano part.
I have studied the score and it is . . . remarkable.

ELLA

Now all we need is the orchestra: 24 first violins, 20 second
violins, 16 violas, 14 cellos, 12 double basses, 4 mandolins, 4
harps, 8 trumpets, 7 trombones, 3 oboes, one organ and a
children's choir.

BETH *takes this in.*

BETH

But I haven't played since I was 18.

ELLA

I'm not asking you to play.

You see . . . because Liz has put her name to it, we have been
given the possibility for some dates. We are also in discussion
with an orchestra and a London choir and that's where you
come in . . .

BETH

How?

ELLA

Money.

BETH *plays nervously with a button on her coat.*

BETH

Ah . . .Yes . . . well . . . of course . . . of course . . . I thought . . .

The button comes off in her hand.

ELLA

Oh, it's come off.

BETH *looks at it.*

ELLA *puts the box down.*

BETH
It's come off.

ELLA *holds her hand out for the button.*

BETH *gives it to her.*

ELLA
Take your coat off. I'll sew it back on for you.

BETH *hesitates.*

BETH
I'm cold.

ELLA
It's boiling hot here now.

BETH *reluctantly takes her coat off. She feels very vulnerable.*

ELLA *looks for a needle and thread.*

BETH
You don't understand. I have no money of my own. I have an allowance . . . but not one that could allow me to sponsor a whole orchestra.

ELLA
Beth, this is your chance. You could make this happen. You could be the enabler. That is a noble role. It would suit you.

BETH *doesn't speak.*

LIZ *takes another piece of clothing off.*

ELLA
I understand that it must be hard for you after decades of stooping, riddled with guilt, to straighten out your frozen backbone without breaking it. To stand up and look ahead of you instead of always up. But don't you want to?

BETH
William says: 'Try to grow straight and life will bend you.'

ELLA
(*surprised*)
Does he?

LIZ
(*under her breath*)
Oh fuck . . .

LIZ *takes her final piece of clothing off and sits now naked at the table.*

ELLA *and* BETH *look at* LIZ *without any surprise.*

LIZ
How did you dream up William?

BETH
My dreams did not include a William.

LIZ
No, I suppose they didn't.

The door opens and a beautiful young man in his early twenties comes in.

ELLA
Ah, Harold, just in time.
You have already met Liz –
You opened the door to her – you let her in.

HAROLD *greets* LIZ *politely.*

HAROLD
Yes. Hello.

LIZ
Hi.

No-one seems to be bothered about her nakedness.

ELLA *now takes* HAROLD *across to* BETH.

ELLA
And Harold, this is Beth.
Beth, this is Harold, my son.

BETH *is speechless. There is an immediate rapport between* HAROLD *and* BETH.

It is love at first sight.

LIZ sips her wine.

ELLA joins LIZ at the table with BETH's coat and, during the next scene, she sews the button on.

> HAROLD
> (*to* BETH)
> Hello.

> BETH
> (*to* HAROLD)
> Hello . . .

HAROLD gently takes BETH's hand and holds onto it.

> BETH
> (*softly*)
> Hello . . .

HAROLD kisses BETH's hand tenderly.

> BETH
> (*whispering*)
> . . . . . .

Silent tears roll down BETH's cheeks. HAROLD looks at her. Neither he nor BETH can speak.

LIZ sips her wine.

ELLA sews.

> LIZ
> (*muttering under her breath*)
> Oh, please . . . no tears . . .

> ELLA
> (*to* LIZ)
> What do you expect?

LIZ doesn't answer immediately.

> LIZ
> So?

ELLA
So.

LIZ
Self-pity. Tears always are.

ELLA
Always . . . ?

LIZ
Always.

ELLA
What's the matter with you?

LIZ
It's embarrassing.

ELLA *looks at* LIZ *sitting there naked.*

ELLA *then finishes sewing on the button and gently turns to* BETH.

ELLA
There we are – that will never come off again.
So, Beth, what do you think?

BETH *can't take her eyes off* HAROLD.

LIZ
She's lost the power of speech.

ELLA
Beth . . . ? About the proposal . . . ?
The money . . . ? What do you think?

Lights fade down.

ACT TWO

Lights fade up.

We hear an orchestra playing part of the second movement of ELLA's piano concerto, as the space is being transformed into a rehearsal studio with a piano, chairs and music stands.

During this transformation, LIZ is changing into a fabulous dress. When it is time for her solo, LIZ sits down behind the piano and plays with great passion.

ELLA enters and sits down on one of the wooden chairs. She listens to LIZ with concentration.

After a while, BETH comes in wearing a summer suit. She tiptoes across the room so as not to disturb the concentration, which she, of course, does.

BETH signs to ELLA that she has the leaflets. ELLA shuts her up with a glance.

BETH finds a chair and sits down. She rummages through her bag.

ELLA gives her another furious glance.

BETH stops rummaging and sits now quite still, pretending to listen to LIZ's playing but her mind is obviously on the leaflets she can't find.

ELLA is totally focused on LIZ.

LIZ plays magnificently.

When LIZ comes to the end of the second movement, there is a complete silence for a while, then BETH starts to clap.

BETH
Brilliant! That's brilliant!

ELLA *gives her another furious look, which shuts her up.*

BETH *returns to rummaging through her bag.*

ELLA *walks over to* LIZ.

> ### ELLA
> (*hesitant*)
> Yeah . . . that's . . . yeah . . .

ELLA *looks at the score and turns to a particular page and studies it.*

> ### LIZ
> You don't like it.

> ### ELLA
> No, no, I do. It's just that . . .

> ### BETH
> I think it's brilliant.

ELLA *looks at* BETH.

> ### ELLA
> Beth . . . please . . .

BETH *goes back to her rummaging.*

ELLA *turns back to the score.*

> ### ELLA
> Here . . . the way you . . .

> ### LIZ
> Yeah, I know, but the top E flat – listen . . . (*she plays it*)
> Where's Harold?

> ### BETH
> He'll be here soon.

ELLA *and* LIZ *look at* BETH. *Then* ELLA *turns back to the score.*

> ### ELLA
> It's the tempo.

> ### BETH
> I like the tempo.

ELLA *desperately tries to ignore* BETH.

LIZ
She likes the tempo.

ELLA
(*studying the score*)
And here . . . the shading . . . Remember: flapping, soaring,
flapping, soaring with neck outstretched and legs trailing. This
here . . . should be . . . delicate, so . . . think of . . . the nuances
of a sigh . . . and here . . . the phrasing . . . you seem to shout.
No-one likes to be shouted at. Why don't you speak? Or better
still, whisper . . .

Pause.

LIZ
This is my interpretation.

ELLA
It's not what I have written.

Pause.

BETH
I've found them.

Neither of the other two react.

BETH
The leaflets, look, I've found them.

ELLA
Not now, Beth please, not now.

BETH *sits there quietly.*

BETH
Now you're dreaming, Beth, now you're dreaming.

Pause.

LIZ
(*to* BETH)
She doesn't like the way I play it.

All three sit in silence for a while. Quite separate.

BETH

I was studying the score yesterday and I was amazed. It all came
flooding back. Don't forget that before we were eighteen we had
already practised more than 15,000 hours. Last night I counted
them. Two hours a day between the age of six and twelve, and
five hours a day between twelve and eighteen.

ELLA and LIZ look at her.

BETH

15,000 hours before eighteen.

They all think about that for a moment.

BETH
(*to* LIZ)
You must have done over 50,000 hours by now . . . at least.

They all think about that.

BETH
(*to* LIZ)
You've won.

LIZ
Won what?

BETH
The crown.

LIZ
Have I?

BETH
You're wearing it!

LIZ radiates as she is wearing her imaginary crown.

BETH
It suits you.

BETH and ELLA look at LIZ.

LIZ
(*to* ELLA)
Bitter, are you?

ELLA doesn't speak.

BETH

William always says: 'Every choice has its future.'

ELLA

William says a lot, doesn't he?

LIZ

(*to* ELLA)

Yes, and he is right.

Every choice does have its future,

and your choice was to have the baby.

BETH *and* LIZ *look at* ELLA.

LIZ

You sacrificed your life for it.

BETH

(*to* ELLA)

You did.

LIZ

(*to* ELLA)

You said you fell in love with it and made it your life's work.

ELLA

What?

LIZ

The baby.

ELLA

I did. And I don't regret it. That choice has made me what I am today.

LIZ

Shrivelled up and spent.

BETH

Liz . . .

Pause.

ELLA

(*to* LIZ)

Just like your choice has made you what you are today:

A whore!

BETH

ELLA . . .

ELLA

(*to* BETH)

She plays to please, to entertain.

BETH

What is wrong with that?
Do you prefer an empty concert hall?

LIZ

She obviously does.

BETH

(*to* ELLA)

I thought you wanted to reach the people, to affect them,
maybe even change them.

ELLA

No. I'm not a missionary.

Pause.

LIZ

(*to* ELLA)

Why don't you stay behind your own piano, then? Or better
still, why don't you stay in your own head? Why have you
spent ten years composing this?

(*to* BETH)

What does she want?

BETH

(*to* ELLA)

What do you want?

ELLA

To be heard and understood.

BETH

Everyone wants that.

LIZ

What?

BETH

To be heard and understood. But nobody is listening.

Pause.

ELLA

Kindred spirits will pick it up,
Non-kindreds will walk past.

LIZ

What?

ELLA

(*to* BETH)

Exactly! She's just proved my point.

Pause.

BETH

The problem would be solved if you would cut this part of the second movement. William thinks it would be better cut and so does Simon. We've been discussing it.

ELLA *is speechless.*

BETH *searches in her coat pocket for cigarettes.*

BETH

We haven't got much time though. The orchestra will be here soon.

LIZ

What did you just say?

BETH

The orchestra will be here soon. You know that.

LIZ

No, before that.

BETH

We haven't got much time.

LIZ

No, something about William wanting this part of the second movement cut?

BETH
He does.

LIZ
How dare he?

BETH
And so does Simon and, as a matter of fact, so do I.

ELLA *and* LIZ *look at* BETH.

BETH
It doesn't work.

ELLA
Cut the stork? Are you deranged? This proves it. This just proves it. You haven't got an inkling what this piece is all about. The stork! The voiceless stork, who flaps and soars throughout the piece. The violins pick up the echo and later on the oboes too. How CAN you? It is the core of the piece – the island in the lake.

> (*she turns in despair to* LIZ)
> How can she? She . . . lunches!!

ELLA *continues in silent agony.*

LIZ
Ignore her.

ELLA
How?

LIZ
We never asked her to join because of her exquisite artistic judgement, did we? She's just the rich bitch who coughs up all the money and in return she may sit in the middle of the front row of the Royal Circle with William by her side, wearing their tiaras.

ELLA
What . . . ? William . . . ?

LIZ
Who knows? I wouldn't be surprised.

ELLA

Really . . . ? God . . . I had no idea . . .

ELLA *looks at* BETH *with different eyes.*

ELLA

William? Fancy that!

ELLA *and* LIZ *turn to each other and convulse into uncontrollable laughter for quite some time.*

BETH *tries to ignore them for a while, then she speaks with dignity.*

BETH

I wonder if you will still be laughing when William withdraws his funds and his contacts? Where will you be then? You won't have Simon, for a start.

LIZ

(*to* BETH)
Without William?

LIZ *turns to* ELLA.

LIZ

She thinks that Simon came on board because of William's purse. She thinks that it has nothing to do with the fact that Simon has known me for ten years and has been dying to work with me.
(*to* BETH)
And you know why?

ELLA

To further his career. We all know it's on the wane.

LIZ

That too.

ELLA

Why else?

LIZ

Because he wants to shag me.
I have the reputation that I shag most of my conductors.

ELLA
Do you?

LIZ
Reputation, I said. But there is no smoke without fire, of course,
as Queen Elizabeth used to say.

BETH
(*totally gullible*)
Oh . . . ? Was it Queen Elizabeth who first . . . ?
Ah yes, of course.

LIZ
(*muttering to herself*)
Oh fuck . . .

BETH
What . . . ?
Did she coin the phrase?

LIZ
What phrase? What are you talking about?

BETH
'There is no smoke without fire.'

LIZ
No, I don't believe she did.
But she was on the throne when London was burning.

BETH
She wasn't.

LIZ
She was.

ELLA / BETH
(*to* LIZ)
She wasn't.

BETH
It was Charles II.

ELLA
It was.

                         BETH
                        It was.

                          LIZ
                      WHO CARES?

Pause.

                         BETH
We'll ask Harold when he comes. He knows everything.

ELLA *and* LIZ *look at* BETH, *each in their own way.*

                         ELLA
               He does seem to sometimes.

LIZ *sighs.*

                         ELLA
                      He does.

                         BETH
                      He does.

                         ELLA
When he was only seven and he couldn't sleep (he could never
sleep as a child), I told him I would give him a magic potion.
And do you know what he said?

LIZ *looks at her watch.*

                         BETH
                      What?

                         ELLA
He said: 'I don't believe in magic. Deep down there's an
answer to everything' . . . he said. 'The trouble is,' he said,
'you can never get deep down' . . . Seven!

BETH *thinks about this.*

                          LIZ
                     Incredible!

                         BETH
                    Trouble . . . ?

ELLA

What do you mean?

BETH

You said he said: 'the trouble is'. Did he seem troubled?

ELLA

As a child?

LIZ

Well, for a start, he could never sleep. Of course he was
troubled. But are you surprised?

They all think about that for a while.

LIZ

So what are we going to do?

ELLA

Well, I was hoping . . . He seems happier now, though . . .
(*she turns to* BETH)
Don't you think?

LIZ

No, about Simon.

ELLA

Oh, I don't like Simon. I want him sacked.

BETH

(*smiles*)

That is not up to you.
Anyway, the leaflets have been printed.

ELLA

He's got to go. He's ruining this piece. He contorts every
phrase by imposing an inner meaning on it, which is untrue
and totally affected. Liz used to play with simplicity. That is
how we were taught: modesty of movement – sobriety of
expression. Never this eagerness to please, this showing off.

BETH

(*quietly to* LIZ)
She thinks you're showing off.

LIZ *takes this in.*

ELLA
(*to* BETH)
All she's interested in are thunderous climaxes!

LIZ
(*to* BETH)
She wouldn't recognise one if it bit her on the lip.

BETH
Wouldn't she?

LIZ
Look at her!

LIZ *and* BETH *look at* ELLA.

ELLA
(*to* BETH)
There's a time and place for everything but Liz crescendoes all the time, out of all proportion, until the music has no meaning left at all. She thinks that louder means stronger, whereas, of course, it dulls. The result is bland and generalised, a perfect dish to serve up to her sycophantic audiences! It stinks.

BETH
(*to* LIZ)
She thinks your playing stinks.

LIZ *gets up from the piano stool and collects her coat, her hat, her scarf, her gloves, her bag.*

BETH
(*to* ELLA)
Now look what you have done.

ELLA
Where are you going?

LIZ
I have some whoring to do elsewhere.

BETH
Don't go.

LIZ

(*to* BETH)

Creators are a rare species.

Interpreters much less so.

It won't be hard for you to find another pianist.

BETH

But the leaflets have been printed and the orchestra will be here soon. You look lovely in that dress. Doesn't she?

ELLA *does not react.*

BETH

She looks lovely in that dress.

(*to* LIZ)

That is definitely the one to wear. You look lovely.

LIZ

(*to* BETH)

Thank you. You're very generous. And before I go, I want you to know that I think that you've got an extraordinary talent for photocopying and the way you lick those envelopes . . .

BETH *is taken aback.*

LIZ

And what you also have, of course, is an infallible instinct.

(*she turns to* ELLA)

She has, you know, and all you need to do, Ella, is listen to her.
Cut the stork! Shoot it!

BETH *is confused.*

BETH

But I thought . . .

LIZ

(*to* BETH)

How can I play this stuff? How can anybody play it?
The Stalking of the Stork.
It's a lie. She hasn't got the nerve to tell the truth.

There is an awkward pause.

LIZ
(*to* BETH)

Do you know why we never saw the stork? Do you?

Because he couldn't wait to go for his fish and chips and ketchup with Auntie Rita! She forgot that bit.

And when we were locked up, it was not crying that we heard – And afterwards, when they did unlock the door and opened it to let us out, their faces were bloated with a mixture of ecstasy and shame. Ella has forgotten that. And how he bribed us with caresses, promises and sweets as long as we kept quiet – and we did. Because we were afraid, it was pure fear. That's why. We kept his secret, and became the mute one, slouching in the corner.

Pause. All three sit slouched in their chairs. It is a chilling moment.

BETH
The trouble is, I can't remember much.

LIZ
She is a liar.

BETH
(*to* ELLA)
She says it's not the truth.

ELLA
She knows it is.

BETH
She doesn't.

ELLA
She does. And so do you.

BETH
The trouble is I have forgotten most of it.
(*to* ELLA)
She says you haven't got the nerve to tell the truth.

ELLA
Does she still believe the truth to be a simple possibility?

BETH

It is, of course it is, otherwise where would we be?

ELLA

From where I am standing and what I am looking at,
it is the Truth.

BETH

It's your interpretation.

LIZ

It's not what has been written.

Pause.

BETH

William says: 'Truth can be attained, if at all, only in silence.'

LIZ

Then why won't he shut the fuck up?

No-one speaks.

LIZ *gets up and puts her hat, gloves and scarf on.*

BETH

She's threatening to leave.

ELLA

She can't.

LIZ *is on her way towards the door.*

BETH

(*to* LIZ)

Please Liz, don't go – we must stay in this together. We are so
nearly there. We have worked hard. We have got a wonderful
orchestra, a great conductor, a brilliant pianist, a . . . score . . .

ELLA *tries to control herself.*

. . . The money is in place – the dates are booked, the leaflets
have been printed – Please, if we stick together, this could be
magnificent –

LIZ *hesitates.*

BETH
(*to* ELLA)

If Liz really thinks that the stork should be cut, and I do and Simon and William, then perhaps it should be.

ELLA

A democratic vote, you mean? That only works if the voters have had some form of education on the matter and in this case I can't see much proof of that. So let the thick majority rule? Simon hasn't got a clue what this piece is all about, you have chosen amnesia and have cut off all connections, Liz is too filled with anger and disgust to hear and William . . . ? What reason does William give to cut the stork?

BETH

He says it's too Romantic.

ELLA

Ah . . . and does sweet William know the meaning of the word?

BETH

'Romantic'? (*she thinks for a moment*) Maybe not.

ELLA

Romantics value the moment . . .

She grabs an imaginary moment and holds it in her hand.

ELLA

. . . even if afterwards it is destroyed, changed or it vanishes.

ELLA *lets the imaginary moment go.*

ELLA

Cynics, on the other hand, don't value anything at all.
I'll never cut the stork.

LIZ *turns to go.*

ELLA

Coward! That's typically you! Abort it!
I should have known you would.

LIZ *turns to face* ELLA.

LIZ

What makes you think abortion was the easy option?

ELLA *doesn't answer.*

LIZ

You ran away!
(*to* BETH)
Do you remember how we lay there on the clinic bed?

BETH

I don't remember anything.

LIZ

You do.

ELLA

Of course you do.

BETH

Do I?

LIZ

(*to* BETH)
Of course you do. We lay there ready for the anaesthetic. Then
suddenly Ella got up and on her bare feet, in her green cotton
night gown, she ran out of the ward, along the vinyl corridor,
down the stony stairs, across the street, even though it was
pouring down with rain, she ran away, screaming and sobbing,
clutching the vile growth in her swollen womb. She ran away.

BETH

She did . . .

LIZ

(*to* BETH)
And then you followed. I was the only one who had the nerve
to stay there and go through with what had to be done: to get
rid of it.

BETH *and* ELLA *look at* LIZ.

LIZ

I did not want that monster's child, not anybody's.

BETH *and* ELLA *have no answer.*

LIZ

Should I have given birth and sacrificed myself for it or other children like Mother did? Why? So that in turn those children could grow up to sacrifice themselves for their children so that in turn those children could grow up to sacrifice themselves for their children until there is nothing left but sacrifice and cowardice?

They all think about that for a moment.

BETH

You were the brave one.

LIZ

I don't object to being called a whore. I don't mind that.
But coward . . .

LIZ turns again to leave.

BETH

Liz! Ella . . . ?

ELLA doesn't stir.

BETH walks towards LIZ.

BETH

You're not a coward. That is the last thing you are. You are the only one of us who still has the nerve to perform in public. To walk that tightrope without safety net. I'd rather curl up and die a painful death than appear on a stage in front of a live audience. Liz . . . you are the brave one . . . please come back . . .

BETH walks LIZ back into the room and sits her down.

BETH

I'll show you the leaflets.

BETH gets the leaflets and they all are seated now.

LIZ
(*to* ELLA)

We were sitting at that oblong table every evening at six o'clock.

BETH

The walls were blue . . . That's all I can remember.

LIZ

The cushions always newly covered. The odd visitor who came.
Mother's frocks and scent, her curls, her face made up, covering
her pain and her anxiety . . . Our mouth was shut.

BETH

. . . There were no mirrors . . .

LIZ

Jane hating her own image, hiding from the world until she left
it. And all because of him, whom you so lovingly have hoisted
high upon a marble pedestal and have absolved from guilt.

Pause.

BETH

He slept a lot, I do remember that.

LIZ

He was bone-idle.

ELLA

He was a dreamer.

Pause.

LIZ

Mother had dreams.

BETH

Everybody does.

LIZ

Yes, but Mother's were big and so the loss of them must have
been big too.

BETH

How can you measure dreams for size?

ELLA

No, they can't be measured.

Pause.

BETH

The man without ambition.

ELLA

He was too intelligent for that.

LIZ

Too lazy.

ELLA

After Jane's death, Mother hid behind religion. 'Because there must be more to life than this,' she said. Whereupon Father cried out in pure wonder: 'MORE . . . ? MORE . . . ?' You see, he was dazzled by a voiceless stork, a floating swordfish, the mystery of the swollen waters of the sea . . .

(*to* LIZ)

You talk of sacrifice, ambition, career, achievement. I know he was no go-getter, but he had that rare ability to see when he was looking, to hear when he was listening, to be, just to be; so gentle, so simple, so pure. Maybe that's what death is like.

BETH

What?

ELLA

Just being.

LIZ

Death is NOT being.

ELLA

Yes, of course, you're right.

Pause.

ELLA

You should have been there when he died.

BETH

We were on holiday.
It would have cost a fortune to fly home.

LIZ

I vowed I'd never set eyes on him again.

Jane was dead and Abigail and Mary didn't bother coming back.

BETH

No, they didn't.

ELLA

I had my left arm around the whole of him like a wing, and
with my right hand I steadied him and helped him . . . across
the threshold . . . he had difficulty breathing . . . His breaths
were like a succession of impulses that converged towards a
definite repose . . . who said that?

BETH

What?

ELLA

'Music is nothing more than a succession of impulses
that converge towards a definite repose.'

Pause.

BETH

It wasn't William, I know that.

LIZ

Thank God for that.

ELLA

Stravinski.

BETH

Who?

ELLA

Stravinski.

BETH

Oh yes, of course. Stravinski.

ELLA

Mother's love was conditional. Sit up and I will love you;
Eat up and I will love you; Practise and I will love you;
Be good and I will love you. But his was unconditional . . .

LIZ

. . . on one condition:
that we kept silent.

ELLA *has no answer to that.*

LIZ
He was a weak man.

BETH
I really don't remember him that well.

ELLA
He was the only man I ever loved.

LIZ
I hated him and always will.

ELLA
You have no heart.

LIZ
And you know why? Because I served mine up to Daddy. I served it on a plate. He covered it in ketchup and stuffed his face with it. It was the only heart I had and now I go without.

No-one speaks for a while.

BETH *collects the leaflets and takes up a position of power.*

BETH
As far as I can see, we haven't got much time before the orchestra arrives and we have two matters to discuss . . .

ELLA
Where's Harold? – I'm getting worried now . . .
He's such a dreamer, sometimes he forgets . . .

BETH
Ella, please . . . He won't be long.
So, two matters. One: the leaflets, and two: the recording rights.

ELLA
What?

BETH
I have clinched a brilliant deal for the concert to be broadcast.

ELLA
You what?

BETH

Yes, with Liz on board and Simon, they were extremely keen.

LIZ

Who?

BETH

There is nothing to worry about. I've signed and sealed it.

BETH *rummages through her papers.*

ELLA

Hang on . . . hang on . . . You act as if you own this.

BETH

I do. I have bought it. It is mine.

ELLA *and* LIZ *are speechless.*

ELLA

(*to* LIZ)

Beth says she owns it.

LIZ

Yes. She DOES.

ELLA

But . . .

LIZ

(*to* ELLA)

You are so naïve. That's how it works: You spend a lifetime
mining the gold. Then I come along, a hired hand, skilled after
50,000 hours of practice. I mould the gold into a ring. Then
she borrows some money from her husband, buys it at cost
price, puts it in a little box and wraps it up in shiny paper. Then
she shouts about it, sells it at a profit, which, of course, is
solely hers. And you thought SHE was gullible?

ELLA *has no answer.*

LIZ

She has learnt quickly, you must admit. It suits her.
She's positively thriving.

ELLA

I preferred her bent, stooping with guilt, and frozen.

LIZ

She doesn't eat the skin of the chicken, she carefully cuts off the fat from the lamb, but, my God, she's greedy for the grease.

ELLA
She wants it all.

LIZ
What's that smell?

BETH
Ella reeking of alcohol.

ELLA *looks at* BETH.

LIZ
No, something rotten.
I wonder what it is?

ELLA *and* LIZ *are sniffing a bad smell.*

BETH
No need for that.

ELLA
(*to* BETH)

To think that if I had chosen your path at that crossing where we stood, I could be standing there, where you are standing now . . . believing I was right.

ELLA *and* LIZ *watch* BETH, *standing where she is standing, for a while.*

BETH
I am.

Pause.

LIZ
You're not.

BETH

If you don't like it then take your bundle of annotated papers, your concerto, and put it safely back in your wooden box, where it will slowly decompose itself . . . until it's nothing . . .

an egg, unfertilised, a sperm that lost its way, a seed that never reached the soil.

BETH *starts to collect her papers and leaflets.*

LIZ
Greed, greed, greed.

BETH
(*quietly*)
Yes, I'm just the rich bitch, who coughs up all the money and in return I can sit in the front row of the Royal Circle wearing my tiara with William by my side. I'm not allowed to have artistic satisfaction. My opinion is always ridiculed. As for financial gain, that is perceived to be obscene. I am obscene. Where as you . . .

BETH *looks at LIZ.*

LIZ
What?

BETH
(*to LIZ*)
To think that if I had chosen your path at that crossing where we stood, I could be standing there, where you are standing now . . . believing I was right.

ELLA *and* BETH *look at LIZ, standing where she is standing, for a while.*

LIZ
I am.

ELLA
You're not.

BETH *starts putting her coat on and collecting her things. Then she turns to* ELLA.

BETH
(*to ELLA*)
You've made Father into a god, but in my dreams he features as a demon. I have this recurring dream: I'm crossing a field. It is freezing cold. I cross it because it is a shortcut. The grass is

frozen. The wind is icy. I stretch my woollen collar to cover up my ears.

From the opposite corner of the field, I see a young father clutching his toddler in his arms. He walks towards me. He has also chosen the shortcut.

He holds his toddler tight. Protecting it from every gust of wind. Our paths cross in the middle of the field. I catch his radiant smile. He can't believe his joy. He squeezes his beloved toddler tightly. He squeezes it to death.

LIZ *and* ELLA *take this in.*

BETH

I DON'T remember the oblong table, every evening at six o'clock. I DON'T remember all his oozing charm, bribing me with chocolate ice-creams and fish and chips with ketchup. I DON'T remember him carrying me up the stairs to bed holding me safe in his strong arms. I DON'T remember him caressing me when I'd woken up with a bad dream. I DON'T remember him stroking my forehead until my headache disappeared. I DON'T remember him standing on his head in the middle of the room to amuse me. I DON'T remember him tickling me until I was weak with laughter. I DON'T remember the gentle way he played his viola. I DON'T remember his conspiring winks across the table saying: I am yours as long as you are mine, manipulation, manipulation, manipulation until Jane killed herself . . . I'm glad I have forgotten it. My youth, my memories of him, my music, I bundled them all up, together with the baby, and gave them all away. I'm glad. All gone.

BETH *walks to the door.*

LIZ *follows her.*

LIZ

Beth, don't go, we're all in this together. You said so yourself.

LIZ *guides* BETH *back and puts her on a chair.*

ELLA

He was shattered after Jane's death. Do you remember what he said that morning, after he'd discovered her on the island?

LIZ

Stop prodding in that stagnant pool.

ELLA

It's not stagnant if you keep prodding it. And I keep prodding it, because I seem to be the designated one to tend the island in the lake.

LIZ

It's an illusion.

ELLA

A living one . . . which is better than your dead reality. Your dead certainties, no room for doubt, no room for any nuances . . .

LIZ *turns away.*

ELLA

He was a broken man. He was so cold, he hadn't slept all night. He had picked up the red beret Jane had left behind. A French one, you know the kind. What do you call it?

BETH

A French Beret.

ELLA

That's it. He was wearing it. He was sitting on the grass. He had been there all night. He hadn't slept. He was smoking one of his cigars. I can smell it now, as always. He was holding it between his long fingers, pressing it to the soft lips of his loving mouth.

BETH

It was a black beret.

ELLA

No, I'm certain it was red.
It left an indelible imprint.

BETH
Indelible?

ELLA
Never to be bleached again.

Pause.

ELLA

'Elizabeth . . . ' he said, can you remember what he said?

LIZ

No.

BETH

I have forgotten.

ELLA

I can't remember either but I can still see him sitting there
blindly staring ahead of him . . . desolate . . . I can still feel his
gentle touch. We were eighteen for God's sake, we were old
enough to know. It wasn't rape, we were consenting adults.

LIZ

After ten years of foreplay, what can you expect?

ELLA

Oh, Liz . . .

LIZ

You disgust me! How you insist on defending him. And what
did Harold say when you told him who his father was?

ELLA *freezes.*

ELLA

He's never asked.

BETH *and* LIZ *look at* ELLA.

ELLA

Once, when he was ten, he wrote a letter, put it in an envelope,
sealed it and addressed it to his father.

LIZ

His father . . . And did you open it?

ELLA

No.

BETH

Did you read it?

ELLA

No.

LIZ
No?

ELLA
No, I didn't.

BETH
But you did give it to his father?

ELLA
No.

They all think about that for a moment.

ELLA
Harold never mentioned it again . . .

LIZ
(*to* ELLA)
Lies, lies, lies . . . To think that if I had chosen your path at
that crossing where we stood, I could be standing there, where
you are standing now . . . believing I was right.

LIZ *and* BETH *are looking at* ELLA, *standing where she is*
standing, for a while.

ELLA
I am.

BETH
You're not.

ELLA
It's odd. Father was the last person who'd imagine himself at
the centre of a story.

They all hover for a moment and end up sitting down on the
chairs scattered around the piano.

No-one speaks for a moment.

ELLA
I am glad I kept his baby, gave birth to it, nourished it and
brought it up to live . . . as Harold . . .

> BETH
> (*muttering*)
> He is very beautiful.

> ELLA
> (*gently*)
> He is.

> LIZ

There are so many 'might-have-beens' in everybody's life.

HAROLD *appears carrying a plastic tray with three plastic cups, a packet of cigarettes, a half litre of whisky and an apple.*

ELLA *goes over to him, she brushes his hair out of his face and wipes some fluff off his jacket.*

The three women look at every movement HAROLD *makes and savour every word* HAROLD *speaks.*

HAROLD *gives a cup to* ELLA *and the whisky.*

> ELLA
> Thank you. Where have you been?

> HAROLD
> I walked, Mum.

> BETH
> You chose to walk?

> HAROLD

Not really chose. It's odd, I just set off and somehow walked here all the way. I got these round the corner.

He hands a cup to LIZ.

LIZ looks at him as he hands her the coffee.

> LIZ
> It's the top E flat – it's sharp.

> HAROLD
> I'll have a look.

He passes a cup to BETH.

He gives a packet of cigarettes to BETH.

BETH
Ah . . .

HAROLD *puts the tray away and carefully polishes the apple. When he has finished shining it, he starts to eat it.*

The women sip their drinks.

HAROLD *eats his apple, core and all, except the stalk. When he has finished he gets up and goes to the piano.*

All three women look at him.

HAROLD *gets down to repairing it.*

BETH
(*tentatively to* LIZ *and* ELLA)
Do you want to see the leaflet?

Pause.

ELLA
(*muttering*)
Alright.

LIZ
(*muttering*)
OK.

BETH *unfolds one of the leaflets and shows it to them. All look at it in silence.*

BETH
You see? The lake . . .
The island . . . The herons . . .

ELLA
No stork . . .

LIZ
No, no stork . . .

ELLA
That's lovely . . .
Look, Elisabeth Faulkener presents –
Big and bold.

ELLA *looks at* BETH.

ELLA
That's you, Beth, aren't you proud?

BETH *is proud.*

ELLA
It's beautiful, well done.

LIZ
And Simon's name up here and mine down there . . . ?

BETH
Yes, you see, design-wise that looked better.

LIZ
Of course, of course. No, that's completely understandable.
That's fine, I can live with that.

LIZ *suppresses her anger.*

ELLA
I don't want to be pedantic but I don't see my name.

BETH
(*pointing it out*)
There, you see, right over the water . . . you see?

ELLA
Oh, yes, I see . . . It's blue on blue . . . yes . . . I can see it now . . .
(*shows it to* LIZ)
You see, there it is . . . sunk into the water . . . blue on blue . . .

LIZ *stands to read* ELLA's *name.*

LIZ
Where?

BETH
It's a lovely colour blue.

ELLA
It is . . . it is . . .

ELLA *suppresses her anger.*

BETH

It was so hard to choose. The possibilities were endless. I knew it had to be the island but from which angle?

And then should we see the stork? Or should we just see a couple of herons or no birds at all?

Should there be clouds or a plain blue sky or should it be night with a sky full of stars?

Then there were so many choices for the lettering – the different fonts, the layout . . . And I thought this was . . . subtle.

LIZ

Subtle?

(*she turns to* ELLA)

Suddenly she decides to be subtle, so subtle that my subtle name has become a subtle, ornamental scroll in the subtle margin, bottom subtle right, and yours has become an oh-so-subtle shadow floating subtly underneath the surface of the water and is only visible when subtly looked at through a subtle microscope. Whereas hers . . . HERS stands out there big and bold, proudly presenting. Presenting what? Who cares?

BETH

Well, William said . . .

LIZ

Fuck William! What do YOU say, Beth?

BETH

I didn't think you'd feel so strongly about a tiny leaflet.

LIZ

You've been wetting your knickers about your tiny leaflet. Ever since you arrived you've been panting to show us your tiny leaflet.

No-one speaks for a moment.

BETH

(*straightening up and standing her ground*)
Well, it has been printed now and distributed.

> ELLA
> Distributed?

> BETH
> Yes.

There is an awkward moment.

LIZ stands up and starts packing her bag.

> BETH

Liz . . . you can't now . . . you'd be breaking your contract.

LIZ looks at BETH but is speechless. Then she looks at ELLA.

ELLA gets up, barely able to conceal her contempt.

> ELLA
> Beth . . . (*but words fail her*)
> Liz . . . I . . .

LIZ and BETH look at ELLA.

ELLA sits down again. No-one speaks.

> LIZ
> So what do we do now?

> ELLA
> Does it matter?

> BETH
> What do you mean?

> ELLA
> It doesn't really matter, does it?

They all think about that for a moment.

> ELLA
> And yet it's all that matters . . .

> HAROLD
> Mum . . .

HAROLD has now repaired the top E flat.

He plays it several times, pure and clear.

The three women look at HAROLD.

HAROLD
Ah, there they are, Mum . . .

They all listen.

HAROLD
More 'might-have beens'.

A female orchestra slowly materialises, playing the second movement.

It consists of: *hippies, who play first violin,*
hookers, who play second violin,
hostesses, who play viola,
librarians, who play cello,
dykes, who play double bass,
nuns, who play the trumpet,
executives, who play the clarinet,
and Muslims in burkas, who play percussion.

When the moment arrives for the piano solo, LIZ *positions herself behind the piano and plays with great subtlety; 'whispering rather than shouting'.*

BETH *and* ELLA, *with* HAROLD *in their midst, sit, watch and listen.*

HAROLD *lights up a cigar, holding it between his long fingers, pressing it gently to the soft lips of his beautiful mouth.*

The music is magnificent.

The End.

Note

The orchestra which appears at the end of the play could be a real orchestra which performs the music live, a symbolic orchestra (i.e. a group of people who represent the idea of an orchestra) or an imaginary orchestra which Harold describes and which the audience perceive only through the reactions of the four actors on stage.